Bear All Year

A Guessing-Game Story

by Harriet Ziefert

pictures by Arnold Lob

Harper & Row, Publishers

Bear likes to play a little every day.
What does he need? See if you can guess.

In the cold of winter Bear likes sledding.
What does he need? See if you can guess.

on my sled.

Watch me zoom down the hill

In the bloom of spring Bear likes running.
What does he need? See if you can guess.

I'm quicker than a bunny in my running shoes.

In the heat of summer Bear likes boating.
What does he need? See if you can guess.

if I tip while I'm boating.

A life jacket will keep me floating

In the chill of fall Bear likes soccer.
What does he need? See if you can guess.

I can kick the ball to the tree!

If I practice,

When winter comes again, Bear likes skating.
What does he need? See if you can guess.

I like slipping and sliding on these skates.

After skating, Bear is cold and tired.

Drink your hot chocolate, Bear.